WHY FEET SMELL

and Other Gross Facts about Your Body

by Jody Sullivan Rake

Consultant: Michael D. Bentley, PhD, Professor and Chair,
Department of Biological Sciences, Minnesota State University, Mankato

CAPSTONE PRESS
a capstone imprint

First Facts is published by Capstone Press,
1710 Roe Crest Drive, North Mankato, MN 56003.
www.capstonepub.com

Books published by Capstone Press are manufactured with paper
containing at least 10 percent post-consumer waste.

Library of Congress Cataloging-in-Publication Data
Rake, Jody Sullivan.
  Why feet smell and other gross facts about your body / by Jody Sullivan Rake.
    p. cm. — (First facts. Gross me out)
  Summary: "Describes unusual bodily functions, including urine, vomit,
and saliva"— Provided by publisher.
  Includes bibliographical references and index.
  ISBN 978-1-4296-7610-6 (library binding)
  ISBN 978-1-4296-7955-8 (paperback)
 1. Microorganisms—Juvenile literature. 2. Bacteria—Juvenile literature. 3. Viruses—
Juvenile literature. 4. Human body—Juvenile literature. I. Title.
  QR57.R36 2012
  612—dc23   2011033929

Editorial Credits
Mari Bolte, editor; Veronica Correia, designer; Marcie Spence, media researcher;
    Kathy McColley, production specialist

Image Credits
Alamy: The Natural History Museum, 21; Capstone Studio: Karon Dubke, 5 (top),
7 (top), 10, 12, 15; Shutterstock: 3445128471, 8, Aaron Amat, 11 (bottom), Arvind
Balaraman, 17 (top), Bill Fehr, 18, Cherry-Merry, 19, Cory Thoman, 14, Damon Ace, 5
(bottom), Dietmar Hopfl, 4, Ecoimages, 13 (bottom), fusebulb, 13 (top), grublee, cover,
Jaimie Duplass, 9 (child), Jakub Pavlinec, 6, Jaroslav74, cover (smoke), 9 (smoke), John
T Takai, 17 (bottom), Kameel4u, 11 (top), Kelly Hironaka, 1, 16, Lorelyn Medina 9
(bottom), Tootles, 7 (bottom), Zametalov, 20

Printed in the United States of America in North Mankato, Minnesota.
102011   006405CGS12

TABLE OF CONTENTS

Slimy Sniffles 4

Why Is Pee Yellow? 6

Facts about Farts 8

Stinky Shoes 10

Good Germs 12

What's Up with Throw Up? 14

Snotty Sneezes 16

Open Wide! 18

Millions of Mites 20

Glossary... 22

Read More.. 23

Internet Sites 23

Index 24

That's So Gross!

Your body is an awesome machine. All the parts work together to help you grow, play, and learn. But your body also makes some pretty gross scents and sounds. Get ready to be grossed out!

Slimy Sniffles

You've got something icky and sticky in your nose. It's a booger! Boogers are made of watery **mucus**. Salt and chemicals make it sticky or slimy. Mucus protects your body from **germs**. Your boogers are usually clear. Thousands of germs inside your nose give boogers their green color.

mucus—a slimy fluid inside a person's nose
germ—a very small living organism

Gross Fact!

Your boogers can be all sorts of colors. They are green and yellow when you're sick. Dirt or dust can turn them black. And red or brown boogers mean you've been picking too much!

Why Is Pee Yellow?

Ever wonder why your pee is yellow? Believe it or not, it all begins with your blood. Old blood **cells** are broken down and moved to your liver. Your liver turns the cells into a yellow liquid. The yellow stuff, called urobilin, leaves your body through your urine. Your pee is actually clear until it mixes with urobilin.

cell—a small, basic unit of living matter

Gross Fact!

The average person passes about 2 pints (.95 liters) of pee a day.

Facts about Farts

Can you smell that? Did someone just fart? **Bacteria** live in your lower **intestine**. They help your body break down food. The bacteria's waste is gas. The gas builds up and needs to come out! Poooot!

bacteria—very small living things that exist all around you and inside you

intestine—a long tube that carries and digests food and stores waste products

Gross Fact!

The average person farts 14 times a day!

9

Stinky Shoes

Keep your shoes on. Your hot, sweaty feet stink! The bacteria living on your skin love that sweat. They feast on sweat, oils, and dead skin cells on your feet. They also produce waste. The waste of a million bacteria is very smelly!

Good Germs

Your body is home to more than 32 million germs. But not all germs are bad. Without good germs, your body could not survive. Some germs help your body break down food and fat. Others can kill bad germs, such as stomach bugs or **infections**. A healthy body has plenty of good germs on hand to help.

infection—an illness caused by germs such as bacteria or viruses

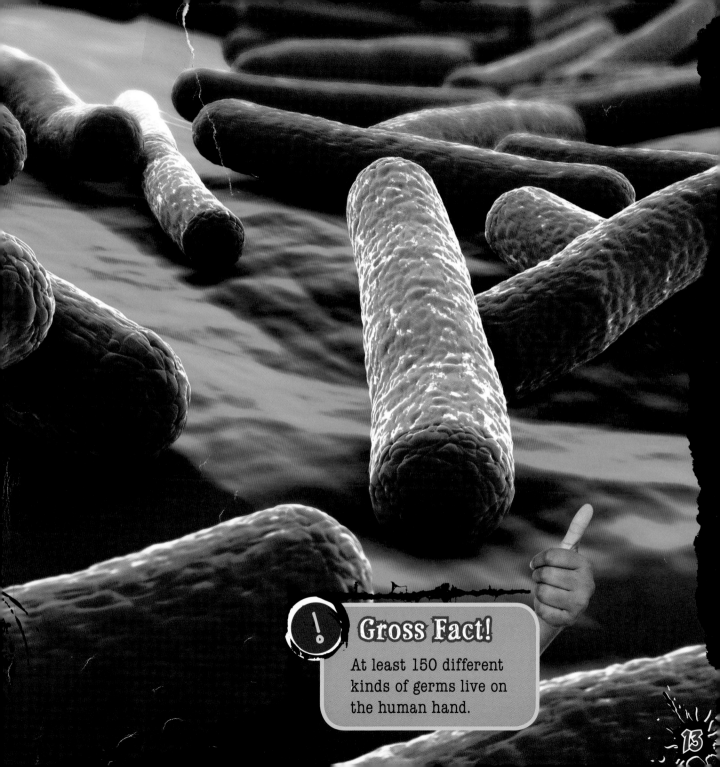

What's Up with Throw Up?

You're looking a little green. Splat! Yuck, you just threw up! Vomit is chewed-up food mixed with stomach juices. Usually your food goes down your throat and into your stomach. But when you're feeling sick, your stomach muscles push the food back up. This action helps your body get rid of whatever was making you feel yucky.

Snotty Sneezes

A sneeze is a high-speed rocket full of germs. When you sneeze, you spray tiny drops of spit and mucus. Thousands of germs are in that spray. Sneezing is healthy for you. It removes harmful bacteria and germs from your body. But don't share snot with your neighbors. Cover your nose and mouth! Ah-CHOO!

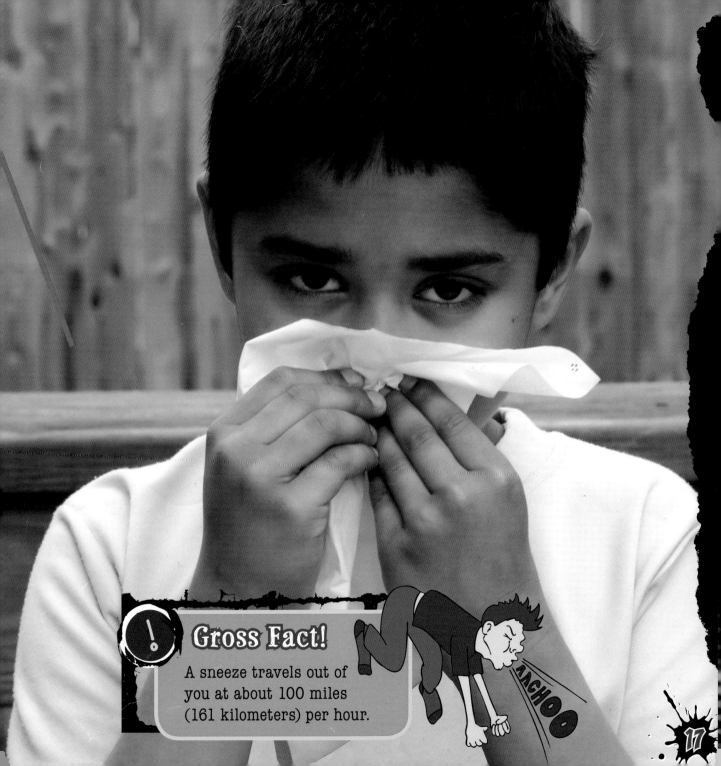

AACHOO

Open Wide!

Need a breath mint? Your friend thinks you do! Germs in your mouth eat bits of food stuck to your teeth and **gums**. They give off waste that makes breath smell bad. The more often you brush and floss, the fewer germs to worry about.

gums—the firm flesh around the base of a person's tooth

Millions of Mites

Your body is crawling with **microscopic** bugs! The tiniest are called mites. Millions of mites live on the hairy parts of your body. But don't worry! Mites are usually harmless. People with a lot of mites might notice the bugs without seeing them. These people are more likely to get zits, mild rashes, and may even lose some hair.

microscopic—so small that it can be seen only with a microscope

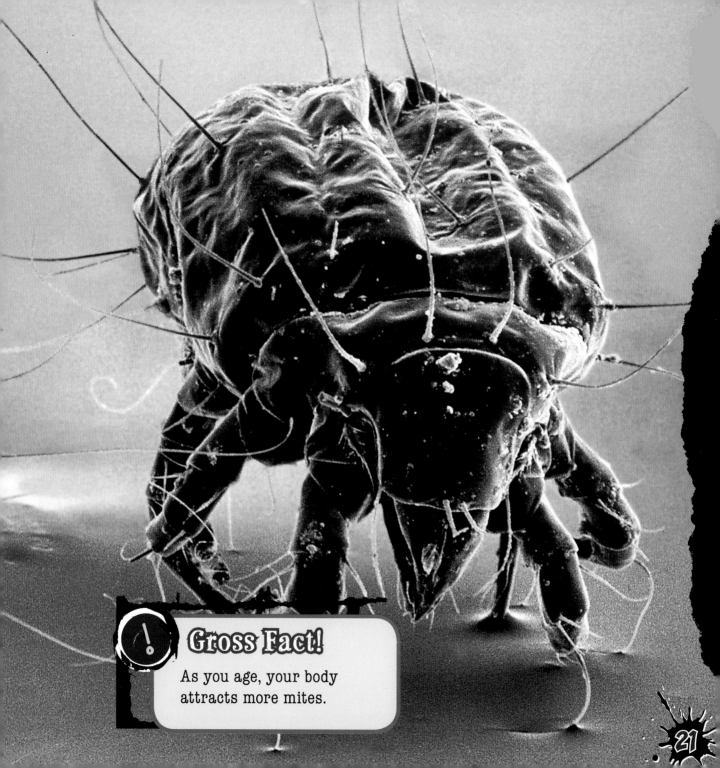

Gross Fact!

As you age, your body attracts more mites.

GLOSSARY

bacteria (bak-TEER-ee-uh)—very small living things that exist all around you and inside you; some bacteria cause disease

cell (SEL)—a basic part of an animal or plant that is so small you can't see it without a microscope

germ (JURM)—a very small living organism that can cause disease

gum (GUHM)—the firm flesh around the base of a person's tooth

infection (in-FEK-shuhn)—an illness caused by germs such as bacteria or viruses

intestine (in-TESS-tin)—a long tube that carries and digests food and stores waste products; it is divided into the small intestine and large intestine

microscopic (mye-kruh-SKOP-ik)—so small that it can be seen only with a microscope

mucus (MYOO-kuhss)—a slimy fluid that coats the inside of a person's breathing passages

READ MORE

Miller, Connie Colwell. *The Pukey Book of Vomit.* The Amazingly Gross Human Body. Mankato, Minn.: Capstone Press, 2010.

Murray, Julie. *The Body.* That's Gross! A Look at Science. Edina, Minn.: ABDO Pub. Co., 2009.

Royston, Angela. *Ooze and Goo.* Disgusting Body Facts. Chicago: Raintree, 2010.

INTERNET SITES

FactHound offers a safe, fun way to find Internet sites related to this book. All of the sites on FactHound have been researched by our staff.

Here's all you do:

Visit *www.facthound.com*

Type in this code: 9781429676106

 Check out projects, games and lots more at
www.capstonekids.com

INDEX

bacteria, 8, 10, 16
blood cells, 6
boogers, 4, 5

cells, 6, 10

farts, 8, 9
food, 8, 12, 14, 18

gas, 8
germs, 4, 12, 13, 16, 18
gums, 18

infections, 12
intestines, 8

mites, 20, 21
mucus, 4, 16

odors, 8, 10, 18

pee, 6, 7

skin, 10
sneezing, 16, 17
sweat, 10

urobilin, 6

vomit, 14

waste, 8, 10, 18